EYE to EYE with ANIMALS

MISCHIEVOUS MONKEYS

by Ruth Owen

WINDMILL BOOKS

New York

Published in 2013 by Windmill Books, An Imprint of Rosen Publishing
29 East 21st Street, New York, NY 10010

Produced for Windmill by Ruby Tuesday Books Ltd
Editor for Ruby Tuesday Books Ltd: Mark J. Sachner
US Editor: Sara Antill
Designer: Emma Randall

Photo Credits:
Cover, 1, 4–5, 6, 7–8, 11, 12–13, 15, 16–17, 19, 20–21, 23, 24–25, 27, 28–29 © Shutterstock.

Library of Congress Cataloging-in-Publication Data

Owen, Ruth, 1967–
 Mischievous monkeys / by Ruth Owen.
      p. cm. — (Eye to eye with animals)
 Includes index.
 ISBN 978-1-4488-8071-3 (library binding) — ISBN 978-1-4488-8107-9 (pbk.) — ISBN 978-1-4488-8113-0 (6-pack)
 1. Monkeys—Juvenile literature. I. Title.
 QL737.P9O93 2013
 599.8—dc23
                                        2012009789

Manufactured in the United States of America

CPSIA Compliance Information: Batch # B2S12WM: For Further Information contact Windmill Books, New York, New York at 1-866-478-0556

CONTENTS

Meet the Monkeys!

They're hairy, they have tails, they live in forests, and they are very good at climbing trees. Meet the monkeys!

Monkeys belong to an animal group known as **primates**. The primate group includes humans, **apes**, monkeys, and **prosimians**, which are small animals such as bushbabies and lemurs. The way to tell monkeys and apes apart is by using their tails. Monkeys have tails—often very long ones—whereas apes, such as chimpanzees, do not.

There are over 250 different **species**, or types, of monkeys. One thing all monkey species have in common is that their **habitat** is being destroyed by their human cousins. Many species are now **endangered** because of habitat loss. So, let's go eye-to-eye with some of the world's most interesting monkeys and find out how they live and what the future holds for them.

Could proboscis monkeys, like the one shown here, be the strangest-looking members of the monkey family?

MONKEY MATTERS

The many different monkey species are divided into two groups—Old World monkeys and New World monkeys. Old World monkeys come from Africa and Asia. New World monkeys come from Central America and South America. Many monkey species live in **rain forests**.

A female white-faced capuchin monkey and her baby

MANDRILLS
Kings of Color

Body length: 22 to 32 inches (56–81 cm)

Tail length: Up to 3 inches (8 cm)

Weight: 25 to 55 pounds (11–25 kg)

Weight at birth: 1.5 pounds (0.7 kg)

Lifespan: Up to 40 years

Breeding age (females): 4 to 8 years

Breeding age (males): 4 to 8 years

Diet: Fruit, seeds, nuts, roots, fungi, frogs, lizards, snakes, snails, worms, and insects

Habitat: Rain forests in Africa

FACE FACTS

Mandrills have red noses and lips, purple and blue ridges on their noses, and golden, furry beards. The more colorful a male mandrill's face, the more attractive he is to female mandrills!

Mandrills are one of the largest species of monkeys. They live in groups of about 20 members, called troops.

Life in the Troop

A mandrill troop is led by an adult male. The leader has the most colorful face in the whole troop. A troop of mandrills spends the day **foraging** for food on the ground. They have large **pouches** inside their cheeks where they can store food for eating later. If plenty of food is available in one place, hundreds of mandrills may gather to eat, forming a supertroop! At night, mandrills climb into trees to sleep.

Mandrill Babies

A female mandrill gives birth to one baby at a time. She feeds the baby with milk and it clings to her fur as she walks around finding food. A baby's aunts and older sisters often help out with childcare. They carry the baby around, too, and play with it.

This fierce-looking face is actually friendly if you're another mandrill!

8

FOLLOW THE LEADER

Mandrills also have red, purple, and blue bottoms. With such colorful bottoms, it's easy to spot the mandrill ahead of you when the troop is moving through thick forests!

A foraging male mandrill with a colorful bottom

Endangered Mandrills
Hunting and habitat loss are the two main threats to mandrills.

Mandrills are hunted to be sold as food, called bushmeat. It's against the law to do this, but hunters still hunt and sell the meat illegally.

The rain forests where mandrills live are cut down for lumber, even though it is against the law.

MANDRILLS RANGE MAP

AFRICA

Cameroon

Congo

Gabon

Atlantic Ocean

The red areas on the map show where mandrills live wild.

A female mandrill and her baby

JAPANESE MACAQUES
Snow Monkeys

Body length: 21 inches (53 cm)

Tail length: 3.5 inches (9 cm)

Weight: 18 to 25 pounds (8.4–113 kg)

Weight at birth: 1.2 pounds (545 g)

Lifespan: Up to 30 years

Breeding age (females): 3.5 years

Breeding age (males): 4.5 years

Diet: Fruit, seeds, flowers, leaves, fungi

Habitat: Forests in Japan

FACE FACTS

Winters are very cold where Japanese macaques live, so they have extremely thick fur. Their faces are a bright pinkish-red color.

Japanese macaque

11

Japanese macaques are nicknamed snow monkeys.
They are often pictured in snow during Japan's cold winters.

Snow Monkey Families

Japanese macaques spend time in trees and on the ground.
They live in troops led by an adult male. Females in a troop form
very strong relationships and **bonds**. They stay in the troop where
they were born for their whole lives. Males leave their birth troop
when they become adults.

Grooming is an important part of everyday life. One monkey
carefully removes **parasites** from another's fur and skin. This helps
the animal being groomed stay healthy. It is also an important way
for the two monkeys to keep the bonds between them strong.

Mothers and Babies

A female macaque gives birth to one baby at a time. Most macaque
mothers feed their babies milk for around six to eight months.
Some mothers feed their babies for over two years.

*A Japanese macaque
grooms a friend
or relative.*

MONKEY HOT-TUBBING

Some Japanese macaques go hot-tubbing in winter to warm up! They spend time in hot springs, or pools of water that are warmed by heat that comes from underground.

Japanese macaques in a hot spring

Japanese Macaques and Humans

There are around 100,000 Japanese macaques living wild.

These monkeys are not endangered, but the forests where they live are being cut down for lumber.

Japanese macaques also eat farmers' crops, so they are in danger of being hunted by people who think of them as a nuisance.

JAPANESE MACAQUES RANGE MAP

China

North Korea

Sea of Japan

South Korea

Japan

Pacific Ocean

The red areas on the map show where Japanese macaques live wild.

A baby Japanese macaque

PROBOSCIS MONKEYS
The Longest Monkey Noses

Body length: 24 to 28 inches (60–70 cm)

Tail length: 20 to 28 inches (50–70 cm)

Weight: 15 to 50 pounds (7–23 kg)

Weight at birth: 1 pound (0.5 kg)

Lifespan: Up to 23 years

Breeding age (females): 4 years

Breeding age (males): 7 years

Diet: Unripe fruit, seeds, young leaves, mangrove shoots; sometimes they eat caterpillars and other insect larvae

Habitat: Mangrove forests, swamps, and rain forests in Borneo

FACE FACTS

The male of this monkey species has a very long, wobbly nose, or proboscis. Scientists think the monkeys' large noses help make their calls sound louder to scare away other males and impress females!

*Adult male
proboscis monkey*

15

Proboscis monkeys spend lots of time in trees. They live in small groups of one adult male and up to seven adult females.

A proboscis monkey high in a tree overlooking a river

Life on the River

Proboscis monkeys live in **mangrove forests** that border rivers. They are very good swimmers. If they want to get to trees on the other side of the river, they leap into the water and swim to the other side. If a river is narrow, they leap from a tree on one side to a tree on the opposite riverbank.

Mothers and Babies

A female proboscis monkey usually gives birth at night, high up in a tree. She has one baby at a time and feeds it milk until it is about seven months old. Young proboscis monkeys stay close to their mothers until they are about a year old.

SWIM FOR IT!

Proboscis monkeys have webbed feet and hands to help them swim well. Moving through the water as fast as possible is important if you're crossing rivers where crocodiles live!

Male proboscis monkey

Female proboscis monkey

These male and female proboscis monkeys live in a protected park. Females have small, upturned noses.

Endangered Proboscis Monkeys

The main threat to proboscis monkeys is habitat loss.

The forests where the monkeys live are cut down for lumber or to make space for farming.

As their homes are destroyed, the monkeys have to come down to the ground and walk long distances to find food and places to live.

PROBOSCIS MONKEYS RANGE MAP

China

Philippines

Malaysia

Borneo

Indonesia

The red areas on the map show where proboscis monkeys live wild.

Baby proboscis monkeys have dark faces until they are around eight months old.

HOWLER MONKEYS
Rain Forest Singers

Body length: 18 to 26 inches (46–66 cm)

Tail length: Approximately 24 inches (61 cm)

Weight: 9 to 22 pounds (4–10 kg)

Weight at birth: 0.3 pound (150 g)

Lifespan: Up to 20 years

Breeding age (females): 3 years

Breeding age (males): 2.5 years

Diet: Mostly leaves but some fruits, buds, and flowers

Habitat: Rain forests in South America

FACE FACTS

Just as their name suggests, howler monkeys can really howl! Their calls can be heard 3 miles (4.8 km) away. Males have special chambers in their large throats to allow them to make very loud calls.

Adult howler monkey

19

Howler monkeys spend all their time in the trees and hardly ever come down to the ground.

A Message for the Neighbors

Howler monkeys live in troops of around five to eight members. Sometimes a larger group of up to 20 members may form. Every morning a whole troop howls together. The group's song tells other troops that live in the same area where that group will be foraging today. The howler monkey troops can then keep some distance between themselves and their neighbors' **territory**. Howler monkeys often howl together in the evening, too, as it starts to get dark.

Howler Babies

Howler monkey females give birth to one baby at a time. They care for their babies for about a year. Other adult females, and sometimes adult males, help care for the baby by carrying it around and grooming its fur.

A howler monkey makes its voice heard!

TWO LEGS AND THREE ARMS!

A howler monkey has a long, strong tail that it uses like an extra arm and hand. It grips branches with this extra "arm" and can even hang from a branch using its tail!

A howler monkey holds tight with its tail while relaxing high in a tree.

Dangers to Howler Monkeys

As more and more rain forest is destroyed in South America, the threat to these monkeys will grow.

Howler monkeys need trees for a place to live. Also, their main food is leaves and howler monkeys need to be able to eat leaves from many different types of trees.

Sometimes howler monkeys are hunted for meat and for their long, thick fur.

HOWLER MONKEYS RANGE MAP

The red areas on the map show where howler monkeys live wild.

A female howler monkey and baby

CAPUCHIN MONKEYS
White-Faced Capuchins

Body length: Up to 17 inches (43 cm)

Tail length: Up to 21 inches (53 cm)

Weight: 4.5 to 9 pounds (2–4 kg)

Weight at birth: 8 ounces (230 g)

Lifespan: Up to 30 years in wild, but can reach 55 years in captivity

Breeding age (females): 4 to 7 years

Breeding age (males): 7 to 10 years

Diet: Fruits, nuts, insects, and sometimes small animals such as squirrels, tree rats, lizards, and birds

Habitat: Many different types of forests in Central America and northwestern South America

FACE FACTS

White-faced capuchins actually have tan-colored skin on their faces. They have a pale ruff of fur around their faces and a "cap" of solid black fur on top of their heads.

White-faced capuchin

23

White-faced capuchins live in groups of up to 20 members. The group includes males and females and is led by an adult male, known as the alpha male.

Capuchin Enemies

Each capuchin group lives in a territory that they defend against other capuchin groups. If an intruder from another group or a **predator** comes close, the capuchins give an alarm call. Sometimes the group will **mob** the intruder or predator to scare it away. Snakes, eagles, and large wild cats, such as jaguars and ocelots, all eat capuchins.

Mothers and Babies

A female capuchin gives birth to a single baby about every two years. She feeds the baby milk and it rides on her back. Female capuchins stay with their mother's group all their lives. Males find a new group to live with when they are about four years old.

White-faced capuchins have tails that are longer than their bodies. They use them for holding onto branches and for carrying food.

ADVENTUROUS EATERS

White-faced capuchins will try almost any food once! They try out new foods and learn through trial and error whether or not something is good to eat.

A female capuchin and her baby

Dangers to White-Faced Capuchins

At the moment, these monkeys are not endangered, but their habitat is under threat.

The forests where capuchins live are cut down for lumber or to make space for farms, leaving the monkeys with fewer places to live.

White-faced capuchins are sometimes hunted by people for food.

These monkeys are also captured from the wild to be sold as pets around the world.

WHITE-FACED CAPUCHINS RANGE MAP

The red areas on the map show where white-faced capuchins live wild.

GOLDEN LION TAMARINS
The Most Endangered

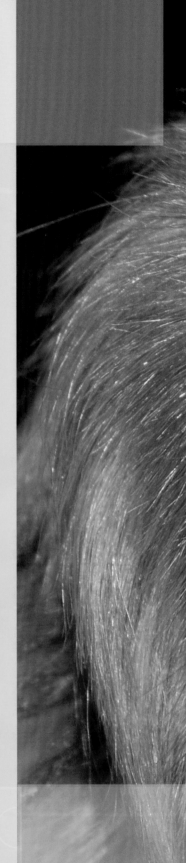

Body length: 8 to 14 inches (20–36 cm)

Tail length: 12 to 16 inches (30–41 cm)

Weight: 23 ounces (654 g)

Weight at birth: 2 ounces (57 g)

Lifespan: 15 to 25 years

Breeding age (females): 1.5 years

Breeding age (males): 2 years

Diet: Fruit, vegetables, eggs, spiders, insects, snails, small lizards and birds

Habitat: Areas of very thick rain forest in Brazil

FACE FACTS

These little monkeys get their name from the thick, golden hair around their heads, which looks like a lion's mane.

Adult golden lion tamarin

Golden lion tamarins live in thick, tangled forest, often 100 feet (30 m) above the ground.

Life in the Treetops

In the daytime, golden lion tamarins climb from tree to tree foraging for food. At night they sleep in holes in trees to stay warm and safe from predators, such as snakes.

Golden Lion Tamarin Families

Golden lion tamarins live in small family groups of up to eight members.

An adult golden lion tamarin and baby

Each family group usually includes an adult male and female, their babies, and their older offspring from previous years. Female golden lion tamarins normally give birth to twins. The mother monkey feeds the babies milk until they are about three months old. The father monkey helps out with childcare and each parent carries one baby on his or her back.

Adult family members spend lots of time grooming and cuddling. The babies like to chase and play wrestling.

FINGER FOOD

Golden lion tamarins have long, thin fingers tipped with little claws. They poke their thin fingers into cracks in tree bark to find insects to eat.

Long, thin fingers

Critically Endangered Golden Lion Tamarins

Golden lion tamarins are one of the most severely endangered primates in the world. There are fewer than 400 left in the wild!

The golden lion tamarin's rain forest habitat is disappearing fast! The trees where they live are cut down for lumber or to clear land for farming.

Thankfully, some zoos are breeding golden lion tamarins. Some of the tamarins raised in zoos have then been set free to live in the rain forest.

GOLDEN LION TAMARIN RANGE MAP

The red areas on the map show where golden lion tamarins live wild.

GLOSSARY

alpha male (AL-fuh MAYL)
The lead male in a group of
animals. Alpha is the first letter
of the Greek alphabet.

ape (AYP) A member of a
group of primates that includes
gibbons, chimpanzees,
bonobos, orangutans, and
gorillas. Apes have no tails, and
most have large bodies. Apes
are very intelligent.

bonds (BONDZ)
Strong, emotional connections.

endangered (in-DAYN-jerd)
In danger of no longer existing.

foraging (FOR-ij-ing)
To move from place to place
looking for food.

habitat (HA-buh-tat)
The place where an animal or
plant normally lives. A habitat
may be a rain forest, the ocean,
or a backyard.

mangrove forests
(MAN-grohv FAWR-ests)
Forests of mangrove trees that
grow in water on the coast in
warm, tropical places.

mob (MAHB)
To scare something by
running at it or crowding
around it, often while making
a lot of noise.

monkeys (MUNG-keez)
Members of the primate group
of animals, such as howler
monkeys or capuchin monkeys.
Most monkeys have small
bodies and long tails.

parasites (PER-uh-syts)
Living things, such as insects
and ticks, that get food by living
on or in another living thing.

pouch (POWCH)
A pocket made of skin.

predator (PREH-duh-ter)
An animal that hunts and kills other animals for food.

primates (PRY-mayts)
Members of the animal group known as primates. The group includes prosimians, monkeys, apes, and humans. Primates are mammals. They are warm-blooded animals that have backbones and hair, breathe air, and feed milk to their young.

prosimians (pro-SIM-ee-inz)
Members of the primate group of animals that includes lemurs and lorises. Prosimians live in forests in Africa, Asia, and on the island of Madagascar.

rain forest (RAYN FOR-ist)
A warm, wooded habitat with a lot of rainfall and many types of animals and plants.

species (SPEE-sheez)
One type of living thing. The members of a species look alike and can produce young together.

territory (TER-uh-tor-ee)
The area where an animal lives, finds its food, and finds partners for mating.

Websites

For web resources related to the subject of this book, go to: www.windmillbooks.com/weblinks and select this book's title.

READ MORE

Gosman, Gillian. *Howler Monkey*. Monkey Business. New York: PowerKids Press, 2012.

Rake, Jody Sullivan. *The Proboscis Monkey*. Weird Animals. Mankato, MN: Capstone Press, 2009.

Somervill, Barbara. *Golden Lion Tamarin*. Road to Recovery. North Mankato, MN: Cherry Lake Publishing, 2008.

Taylor, Marbara. *Apes and Monkeys*. Science Kids. New York: Kingfisher, 2008.

INDEX